MW01281807

About the Authors

Dominic is a local pastor and chaplain. He married up. Jena is a mental health counselor (a big contributing factor to how she can put up with Dominic). We live in Portland, Oregon with our two beautiful daughters.

We've come to realize that over the years we have been trained and equipped in unique ways- many of which we could have never anticipated. Dominic has worked in homeless ministry, addiction recovery, and spiritual formation. Jena's work focuses on issues concerning sexuality, trauma, and spiritual development. The combination of these experiences and skills has developed in us a deep passion for helping others intimately connect with Jesus, in order to facilitate a true understanding of their identities as sons and daughters of the King. The Enneagram has served us well as a tool for our own spiritual growth as well as increasing our ability to understand and connect with others. Consequently, we've become enthralled with how to encourage the use of this tool in the lives of everyone willing to give it a chance.

Introduction

Welcome to the EnneaDevotion! Our hope is that this guide will help you engage the Advent season in a new and personal way. As you encounter Jesus and what he offers you, may you feel accepted for who you are and challenged to grow in the unique ways God has laid out for you. How to use this book: The intent of this devotional guide is to help you experience the four traditional themes of Advent- peace, love, joy, and hope- as you pursue spiritual transformation by exploring your beliefs, engaging your feelings, and moving to action. We will, together, spend a week on each theme. Each day contains a scripture, a general reflection and an Enneagram-specific reflection for each type. Every 6th day, we have provided a day for rest and reflecting on the central theme of the previous week. You will find a brief guide for meditating on these days.

Theological approach to this book:
All too often, Christian devotional life gets quarantined to the realm of the intellect. How much you know, what you can memorize, and what you understand.

As we grow in maturity in Christ, we realize that intellect alone does not equate to holistic holiness. God's desire is that we would be conformed to the image of Christ by the power of the Holy Spirit, for the sake of the world (2 Cor 3:18). To that end, we are called to submit to the powerful work of the Holy Spirit who transforms us on every level.

This devotional seeks to address your mind (beliefs), emotions (feelings), and behaviors (actions) through the power of Word and Spirit. Each part of your being is summoned to behold the beauty of Christ; to be transformed toward that same glory that met us in Bethlehem. It is our sincere hope that you come away from this season being holistically transformed by encountering our Savior in transformative and powerful ways. Discovering your Enneagram type: If you already have an Enneagram type with which you identify, you're all set! Jump right in on December 1. If you haven't yet discovered your dominant type, here are a few steps you can take:

1. Read the brief descriptions of each type on The Enneagram Institute website: www.enneagraminstitute.org
2. If this does not illuminate your type, or if you remain unsure, you can take the Rheti inventory on the same website for $12.

Other helpful resources:
The Sacred Enneagram by Chris Heuertz
The Enneagram: A Christian Perspective by Richard Rohr
The Wisdom of the Enneagram by Don Riso and Russ Hudson
The Road Back to You: An Enneagram Journey to Self-Discovery by Ian Cron and Suzanne Stabile

Prayers

These prayers are included for you to use at the beginning and end of each day's reflection, as a way to surrender yourself to God and His work as you meditate on truth.

OPENING INVOCATION:
O God, who created us in your image,
Grant us grace to see the Imago Dei within our souls.
Remove from us our sin, shame, and sorrow,
That we might celebrate the joy of your presence.
In the holy gift of Jesus in Bethlehem
Let us see your face,
And be transformed from glory to glory,
As we behold the face of our beloved Savior.
Amen.

CLOSING BENEDICTION:
Lord, your eyes see us, your heart knows us, and your arms embrace us.
May your Holy Spirit reveal truth to our hearts.
Comfort us, convict us, and conform us into your glorious image!
We ask all these things
In the name of the Father, the Son, and the Holy Spirit.
Amen.

Peace

This first week of Advent, we'll focus our attention on the theme of Peace. As we explore our beliefs, feelings, and actions together, allow yourself to stay centered on the idea of peace and in what ways you need to feel the peace of Christ this Christmas.

December 1

Isaiah 9:2; 6-7

The people who walked in darkness
Have seen a great light;
Those who dwelt in a land of deep darkness,
On them has light shone…
For to us a child is born,
To us a son is given; And the government will be upon his shoulder,
And his name shall be called Wonderful Counselor, Mighty God,
Everlasting Father, Prince of Peace. Of the increase of his
government and of peace
There will be no end, On the throne of David and over his kingdom,
To establish it and to uphold it With justice and with righteousness
From this time forth and forevermore. The zeal of the LORD of hosts
will do this.

Reflection
Darkness is often an intimidating thing. It is disorienting and
confusing, limiting our ability to know and execute the next move.
Darkness steals our vision and incites fear. But according to Isaiah,
darkness is necessary. Without it, we would never have, nor
appreciate, the dawn and all that dawn brings- peace, warmth,
clarity. What darkness do you see in yourself this Advent? What
darkness do you see around you? How are you interacting with or
opting out of engaging that darkness?

Exploring Belief

Psalm 139:12 speaks of God and says, "the darkness is not dark to you; the night is as bright as day."

Ones: What beliefs are preventing you from moving into a place of peace with God where you enter into the darkness, unable to see what comes next, unable to know what is out of place, yet trust in the God who is your vision?

Twos: What parts of yourself do you see as "dark" or unloveable? What would it take to believe that you are fully loved, despite these dark places?

Threes: In the midst of darkness in and around you, not knowing how to perform or meet the expectations of others, what beliefs stop you from seeing your God-given inherent worth?

Fours: What beliefs about yourself, God, or the darkness you experience prevent you from knowing that you are special and have identity in Jesus?

Fives: For a Five, darkness can feel particularly frustrating as it represents uncertainty, not having all the information. What might it look like to trust God's omniscience even in the darkness, rather than needing to know all for yourself?

Sixes: When you think of being in darkness (physical, emotional, mental or spiritual), what fears surface? How do those fears prevent you from trusting that God is good and has authority, even over the darkness?

Sevens: For a Seven, darkness can represent unmet needs, even the need for light and ability to see. What would it be like for you to sit in the darkness, recognize the needs you have, and trust that God will satisfy those needs? Allow yourself to practice this in this moment.

Eights: Darkness intensifies the feeling of being out of control for the Eight. In what ways is God asking you to relinquish your need for control, and rest in the truth that he is in control?

Nines: When you desperately want to be seen, like many Nines do, darkness can feel like it is working against you. How can you lean into the truth that God sees you and values you even when it feels like darkness surrounds you?

Journaling Space

December 2

Matthew 1:18-23

Now the birth of Jesus Christ took place in this way. When his mother Mary had been betrothed to Joseph, before they came together she was found to be with child from the Holy Spirit. And her husband Joseph, being a just man and unwilling to put her to shame, resolved to divorce her quietly. But as he considered these things, behold, an angel of the Lord appeared to him in a dream saying, "Joseph, son of David, do not fear to take Mary as your wife, for that which is conceived in her is from the Holy Spirit. She will bear a son, and you shall call his name Jesus, for he will save his people from their sins." All this took place to fulfill what the Lord had spoken by the prophet:

"Behold, the virgin shall conceive and bear a son,
And they shall call his name Immanuel."

Reflection

The events surrounding Jesus's conception and birth are pretty wild. Have you ever imagined what it might have been like to be Joseph? A completely mind-blowing, life-changing thing is happening, you've been chosen to be a central figure in it and it comes laced with a high probability of being met with shame and judgment from everybody around you. Stepping forward into this, and responding the way Joseph did, required utter faith in God and a deep understanding of his own identity. He had to trust in the truth of the name given to this baby- Immanuel, God With Us- in order to have peace in a truly impossible situation. What would it take for you to have this kind of belief in God With Us? Are there beliefs about God or about yourself that prevent you from fully accepting the peace that is offered through Immanuel? Acknowledge these beliefs now and present them to Jesus. He wants to address them with you and give you what you need to move forward in confident belief in his peace.

Exploring Belief

Ones: Today, examine your beliefs about what is "right" and what you need to fix about yourself, about others, about the world. As you release these things, welcome the peace that comes through Immanuel as the answer to your striving.

Twos: Today, examine your beliefs about what makes you unloved or even unloveable. As you release these things, welcome the peace that comes through Immanuel as the answer to your striving to earn love.

Threes: Today examine your beliefs about what gives you worth. As you release these things, welcome the peace that comes through Immanuel as the antidote to needing to manage others' perceptions of you.

Fours: Today examine your beliefs about what makes you significant. As you release these things, welcome the peace that comes through Immanuel as the answer to your desperate search for meaning.

Fives: Today examine your beliefs about how your competence staves off feelings of helplessness. As you release these things, welcome the peace that comes through Immanuel as the answer to your quest for knowledge, understanding and resources.

Sixes: Today examine your beliefs about what ensures that you have the support you think you need. As you release these things, welcome the peace that comes through Immanuel as the answer to your anxiety and fear.

Sevens: Today examine your beliefs about how to ensure your needs are met. As you release these things, welcome the peace that comes through Immanuel as the answer to your planning and quest for the "next thing."

Eights: Today examine your beliefs about what keeps you safe and in control. As you release these things, welcome the peace that comes through Immanuel as the answer to your drive to self-protect and maintain control.

Nines: Today examine your beliefs about who you are and what gives you identity. As you release these things, welcome the peace that comes through Immanuel as the answer to your need to "opt out."

Journaling Space

December 3

Micah 5:4-5a
And he shall stand and shepherd his flock in the strength
of the LORD,
In the majesty of the name of the LORD his God. And they shall
dwell secure, for now he shall be great
To the ends of the earth. And he shall be their peace.

Reflection

As God reveals his love for his people, the Bible consistently uses
images of shepherding: God, the Good Shepherd, comes to care for
his people, the sheep of his fold. If we are to receive the blessing of
being shepherded by God, we must come to the humble realization
that we are sheep. While cute and loveable, we are also
defenseless and directionless. To fully embrace the freedom,
power, and peace of God, we are called to remember our great
need for him. Our Shepherd does his work best when we
understand our vulnerability, weaknesses, and fears. What is an
area of your life in which you feel you need God's presence and
peace? In what ways is God inviting you to come under his care as
Shepherd of your soul? Speak with him now, and ask for God's
peace to fill your soul as you cast your cares on him.

Engaging Feeling

Eights, Nines, & Ones: As members of the gut center, Eights, Nines, and Ones benefit from checking in with their physical selves. When you think about God shepherding you into His peace, what do you notice in your body? Spend some time asking Jesus to help you feel his peace in your physical being.

Twos, Threes, & Fours: As members of the heart center, growing in awareness and validation of feelings is particularly important to growth. What feelings are evoked when you picture Jesus as the Good Shepherd offering you his peace? Practice acknowledging and validating whatever feelings come up for you in this time.

Fives, Sixes, & Sevens: As members of the head center, engaging feelings can sometimes seem difficult. However, thoughts can be a strongly-linked channel to your feelings and can help you connect with this part of yourself. As you think about God's peace, offered to you by Jesus the Good Shepherd, ask for help in connecting your thoughts to your feelings. What do you notice?

December 4

John 14:27

Peace I leave with you; my peace I give to you. Not as the world gives do I give to you. Let not your hearts be troubled, neither let them be afraid.

Reflection

Since the Fall in Genesis 3, sin corrupted everything in all of creation- our bodies, our relationships, even Creation itself. Eden went from being paradise to a place of unrest and death. From the time Adam and Eve took their first steps out of the Garden, they (and all of humanity with them) have been in a constant state of searching for the peace that was robbed from them. The shalom and peace that Jesus accomplished permeates every part of what was corrupted by sin. While sin entices you to fear, God's peace invites you to trust and rest. Where in your life are you in need of God's shalom this Advent season?

Engaging Feeling

Ones: As Christmas approaches, are you feeling peace-filled or are you striving to make everything go according to plan? Take a minute and a few deep breaths to center your heart on the peace that Jesus offers, peace that cannot be worked for or earned, but rather is a perfectly satisfying free gift.

Twos: This season can be filled with thinking about others and doing things for others. But Jesus' gift of peace is something he wants to give you simply because HE loves YOU. Give yourself some space now to let this truth sink in and enable you to rest in his peace.

Threes: What does it feel like when peace is found not in being who you think others need you to be but simply in Jesus himself? Take some time to focus your energy on this kind of peace and allow it to be what drives you today.

Fours: The peace that Jesus offers has the capacity to bring emotional balance to the internal chaos Fours often feel. What prevents you from feeling this sort of peace? Once you've identified this, take a moment to center your feelings on Jesus' peace- total fulfillment, shalom.

Fives: The plan that God came up with to bring salvation to the world seems crazy and hard to understand. In what areas are you striving to have complete knowledge? Today, can you take hold of the peace Jesus offers you even without having a full understanding of his plans for you and the world around you?

Sixes: Peace, for the Six, can facilitate setting aside all the lists and contingency plans and letting God's good plans for you take root. Imagine yourself being covered over by this peace, like a wave washing over you. How does this change how you feel about the things you know you will face today and in this season?

Sevens: The kind of peace Jesus offers is called shalom and implies a total satisfaction or fulfillment. When was the last time you remember feeling truly peaceful in this sense? Take some time to imagine yourself receiving Jesus' gift of peace and breathing in the utter fulfillment only he can give.

Eights: God's peace has the ability to help you lay down your self-protective armor. Take a minute to become aware of the areas in yourself that are lacking this peace. Then, ask God to make his peace known to you and to draw you out of your self-protective stance. What does it feel like to freely accept this higher form of peace?

Nines: Nines often describe themselves as feeling like they are asleep to the world and to themselves. Today Jesus offers you a kind of peace that allows you to wake up to who God has created you to be and to embrace your true identity as his son or daughter. How might embracing this kind of peace change your outlook this Advent season?

Journaling Space

December 5

Matthew 5:8
Blessed are the peacemakers, for they shall be called sons of God.

Reflection

Not everyone considers themselves peacemakers and yet if we are children of God, we are called to be peacemakers. While this may seem difficult, there is actually an invitation here. This beatitude from Jesus does not declare blessing over those who are peace-keepers, but those who are peacemakers. Jesus is not celebrating those who keep the status quo, but rather, those who are willing to do what it takes to make peace in areas of chaos. Making peace is not a passive thing. Rather, making peace implies action. What kind of action might God be inviting you to take as you seek to bring about more of his peace in the world this Christmas season?

Moving to Action

Threes, Sevens, & Eights are considered active energy types[i]. These types possess a natural strength and assertiveness. How can your gifts of assertiveness, directness, and strength bring about the peace that this season represents? Spend some time in prayer asking God to direct your strength toward others who so deeply need God's peace in their own lives.

Fours, Fives, & Nines are considered receptive energy types. There is a natural ability for you to understand others' perspectives and bring people together. During this Advent season, the season of peace, how can you take up the mantle of peacemaker using your receptive energy to represent Jesus to those around you? Spend a few minutes asking God to allow your receptiveness to others to become an invitation into relationship with Him.

Ones, Twos, & Sixes are considered balancing energy types. This means that those dominant in one of these types have the ability to make adjustments as necessary in whether to be more active/assertive or more receptive in regard to people and events around them. Advent can be a time where things often feel out of balance. How can you channel your balancing energy in order to bring about a greater experience of God's peace for both yourself and others? Spend some time in prayer asking God to reveal to you places where balance is needed to help facilitate your or another's experience of God's peace.

December 6

Psalm 46:10
"Be still and know that I am God. I will be exalted among the nations, I will be exalted in the earth!"

Today is a day for resting in the knowledge of God and reflecting on his peace. Take a few minutes to quiet your mind, your heart, and your body. Imagine holding yourself up to the warmth of the light of God in order to fully experience God's peace. Spend a few moments there, taking in all that God has to offer you today.

Love

This week, we'll focus our attention on the theme of Love. As we explore our beliefs, feelings, and actions together, allow yourself to stay centered on the idea of love and in what ways you need to experience Christ's love this Christmas.

December 7

Isaiah 54:10
"For the mountains may depart
And the hills be removed, But my steadfast love shall not depart from you
And my covenant of peace shall not be removed."
Says the LORD, who has compassion on you.

Reflection

This Advent season, we have the opportunity to remember God's faithfulness. God's faithfulness is shown in promise after promise through the prophets - He will come near. He will shepherd his people. He will remove our sins as far as the east is from the west. It is God's faithfulness that called Him out of the eternal bliss of Heaven, the unbroken joy of Trinitarian fellowship, and the eternal praises of angelic beings. It was faithfulness that prompted God to humble himself and take our sinful flesh upon himself. It was God's faithfulness that led the Prince of Heaven to be born to poor, humble parents in an animal stall, and to be placed in a feeding trough. But what is the root of this faithfulness? What force could possibly motivate God to take such drastic action? Love. It is because he loves you. God gave up everything because he would rather be with you in the darkness of this world than enjoy the bliss of heaven without you.

Exploring Belief

Ones: Ones often criticize themselves for not measuring up or berate themselves for being unable to "earn" the kind of love and faithfulness that God gives. What false beliefs do you hold about yourself that keep you from fully accepting God's love?

Twos: Love, both giving and receiving it, is of particular importance for Twos. Yet it's common for those dominant in Twos to feel like they must gain the love of others (God included) by first sacrificing themselves to the point of utter self-abandonment. How do your beliefs about how you obtain love prevent you from allowing Jesus to love you freely and without condition?

Threes: Threes work really hard to ensure that others around them like what they see, and that this is the merit that helps them progress in life. Yet, this Scripture promises that, no mater what, God's love for you will always stand. What beliefs do you hold that prevent you from accepting that God sees you as worthy of his love, just as you are without any front or facade?

Fours: In the search for meaning and significance, Fours often get caught in the emotions of the disappointments and heartaches of life. God's promise that his love will never depart from you holds true even when life feels overwhelming and filled with suffering. What would it take for you to shift your focus away from your idea of what love looks like and accept God's love on his terms?

Fives: Fives live with the temptation to hoard their resources so as not to end up feeling helpless or dependent on others. The example set by God, however, as he executed his plan to save humanity shows us just the opposite. He held back nothing, not even his own son, and continues to freely offer all he has to us. How can you set aside your belief that you must be sufficient in and of yourself in order to take hold of the overflow of God's love for you?

Sixes: Fear is the antithesis of love (John 4:18), and for Sixes, it is easy for fear to become the main voice that drives beliefs, and ultimately, behaviors. In what ways is fear driving your beliefs and blocking God's steadfast love from being your source of comfort and certainty?

Sevens: God's love is certain and never-changing. For Sevens this steadiness may seem uncomfortable, and at the same time is exactly what is needed to navigate the pain and discomfort in life. What beliefs fuel your drive to run away or on to the next thing, rather than stilling yourself in God's relentless love for you?

Eights: The love that God offers is significant to Eights as it speaks directly to that part of you that tries to maintain power in every situation. As you read that God's love remains strong and steady even when mountains fall away, what beliefs about your own power need to be set aside?

Nines: Nines often feel as though they can easily fade into the background, and in many ways this is comfortable and easy. They'd rather not "rock the boat" or draw attention to themselves. As you reflect on the ideas of love and faithfulness, what beliefs do you need to give up about your place in this world and your ability to be seen and heard? Is it possible that God is faithful even to you, and might desire the same faithfulness in return?

Journaling Space

December 8

John 3:16
For God so loved the world, that he gave his only Son, that whoever believes in him should not perish but have eternal life. For God did not send his Son into the world to condemn the world, but in order that the world might be saved through him. Whoever believes in him is not condemned, but whoever does not believe is condemned already, because he has not believed in the name of the only Son of God.

Reflection
As people prepare for Christmas, gift-giving becomes a central theme for most of us. Beyond the pressure to shop, spend money, and try to meet the expectations of others there is something deeper happening. At the heart of it, most people want to show their love for others through the gifts they give. And we believe that the better the gift, the better expression of love for another. As we prepare our hearts for Advent, let us take this opportunity to remember the catalyst for our gift-giving. It is a small reflection of the most precious gift that was given to humanity at Christmas: Jesus Christ, the Son of God. If what we believe is true, if the quality of the gift reveals the love of the giver, how much must God love you?

Exploring Belief

Ones: In what ways does God's love offer you a reprieve from the constant internal criticism and drive to be better and do better? Can you allow God's love for you to speak to this part of who you are today and encourage you to accept yourself as you are?

Twos: In what ways is God's love surprising to you? Perhaps its the fact that he actually loves you, perhaps it's that he loves you despite your own feelings of not loving him well enough. What would it mean to you know without any doubt that Jesus loves you? Can you imagine how this might change you?

Threes: God's love invites you to take off your many masks and express yourself as you truly are, knowing that you will still be loved. In some ways, presenting yourself to God as you actually are is a gift you can give him. Can you think of a time when you have done this in the past? What happened? What do you think might happen if you did this today?

Fours: When God looks at you through the lens of his love (which he always does) he sees so much beauty and meaning. He has a plan for you that is truly best for you, even when it doesn't seem to make much sense. What would happen if you accepted this truth today and throughout this Christmas season?

Fives: God's love ultimately leads to connection, both with him and with others. While this might seem scary or intrusive, connecting with others is one of the ways God has given us to learn, grow, and experience. Can you allow God's love to lead you toward others in deep, intimate community? What fears are holding you back from experiencing love in this way?

Sixes: As a master threat-forecaster, you are skilled at doing all you can to keep yourself and those you care about safe. Who or what are you holding at an arm's length in an attempt to protect yourself? What would it mean for you to trust that God's love will protect you and enable you to let others close to you?

Sevens: In Zephaniah 3, God tells his people "I will quiet you with my love." In many ways, this feels like the most intimidating and yet most necessary thing for those who identify with Sevens. Instead of striving to meet your own needs and avoid the pain of deprivation, God's love for you enables you to rest, become introspective, and look for answers to your struggles, rather than running from them. What do you need today to know that God loves you and wants to give you this kind of quiet?

Eights: When you're honest with yourself, you've spent most of your life believing that you are vulnerable and others (perhaps even including God) want to hurt you. Sometimes this backfires though because you also end up keeping out those who want to love you. Can you welcome God's love into yourself today? Can you trust that he doesn't want to hurt you or control you, but rather do what it truly best for you?

Nines: God's love has a unique invitation for you today. It invites you to see and value yourself, to acknowledge your desires and fears, and to take honest action in whatever ways you've felt unable to. Can you embrace that God sees you and loves you, and therefore gives you the ability to see and love yourself?

Journaling Space

December 9

Ezekiel 34:11-15

"For thus says the Lord God: Behold, I, I myself will search for my sheep and will seek them out. As a shepherd seeks out his flock when he is among his sheep that have been scattered, so will I seek out my sheep, and I will rescue them from all places where they have been scattered on a day of clouds and thick darkness. And I will bring them out from the peoples and gather them from the countries, and will bring them into their own land. And I will feed them on the mountains of Israel, by the ravines, and in all the inhabited places of the country. I will feed them with good pasture, and on the mountain heights of Israel shall be their grazing land. There they shall lie down in good grazing land, and on rich pasture they shall feed on the mountains of Israel. I myself will be the shepherd of my sheep, and I myself will make them lie down, declares the Lord God.

Reflection

People have a way of messing things up... us included. The context of this passage speaks of God's displeasure with how Israel's leaders had come to abuse the people rather than shepherd them. The leaders had lost sight of their role and responsibility to love and care for Israel and had become entitled, abusive, and lazy. And in this prophetic passage, God speaks a promise through the mouth of Ezekiel: God Himself is coming to save his people. God vows to step into space and time in order to rescue his people with his own two hands. In the manger at Bethlehem, he made good on his promise. And what greater act of love is there than that? Yet we are left wondering why God would choose to rescue in such a way. He did not come with the authority and power of royalty. He didn't come with vengeful, militant force. He didn't come with religious or institutional influence. He came as a vulnerable, helpless child. And in humility, we surrender and acknowledge that God doesn't make mistakes. His plan was perfectly executed, flying in the face of human wisdom and propriety. This Advent season, we are invited into tension: God's promises (and even his love) may not look like we expect them to look. God chose to enter the world where only the shepherds, the stars, and barn animals celebrated with the holy family. God came to rescue the world by being with us rather than fixing every problem. God wins eternal life and unending glory by dying a humiliating death on a cross. God is the God of the unexpected, yet he is faithful and true. Can you open yourself up to the mysterious ways God may be entering into your world in unexpected ways? It may not make sense to you or this world, but God is intentional and knows what he is doing.

Engaging Feeling

Eights, Nines, & Ones: How can you surrender your body to love today? Take some time to notice anything that feels tense, stiff, or just "off" about your physical self. As you offer these parts of yourself to God, take a few deep breaths and ask God what his love wants to say to you in this moment.

Twos, Threes, & Fours: Your ability to feel deeply is a gift. Today enter into the feeling of being loved and of loving. Think of a symbol that represents love for you and hold it in your mind as you sit in the quiet. Take several deep breaths as you contemplate this symbol and allow yourself to feel deeply God's love for you and your love for him.

Fives, Sixes, & Sevens: Think of a time when you felt most loved by God. Recall as many details of that experience as you are able and hold the picture of that memory in your mind. Take a few deep breaths as you allow yourself to steep in this love and ask God for more moments like this, when you are certain of his love for you.

December 10

1 John 2:28-3:2
And now, little children, abide in him, so that when he appears we may have confidence and not shrink from him in shame at his coming. If you know that he is righteous, you may be sure that everyone who practices righteousness has been born of him. See what kind of love the Father has given to us, that we should be called children of God; and so we are. The reason why the world does not know us is that it did not know him. Beloved, we are God's children now, and what we will be has not yet appeared; but we know that when he appears we shall be like him, because we shall see him as he is.

Reflection
It has been said that, aside from the Gospel, shame is the most powerful force in the world. Shame keeps us on the defensive, always looking for the weaknesses and flaws in others. Shame tempts us to be superficial, hiding our flaws and our true vulnerable nature. Shame traps us, preventing us from growing into the person God has always meant for us to be. But shame is disarmed by the loving acceptance of God through Jesus Christ. The Father has declared that we are his children. While we were sinners, God forgave us and adopted us to become sons and daughters of the King of Heaven. Shame is disarmed when we choose to see our identity in the powerful hands of God, our Father, Rescuer, and Defender. While we await the second advent, the end of all sin and shame, can you embrace your identity as a beloved child of God?

Engaging Feeling

Check in with your body. When you pay attention to what it feels like to experience shame, what do you notice happening physically?

Ones: As a One, you may feel the heaviness in your chest or stomach that represents your ever-present and active inner critic. Perhaps you feel this in some other way or body part. Notice those feelings and invite God's love to replace them with warmth and approval that comes from his love.

Twos: As a Two, shame might feel like an aching in heart as you long to be loved and have your needs met but are not allowed to ask for such things. Ask God to remove this shame and envelope your heart with his perfect love.

Threes: As a Three, shame might be telling you that you're a fraud, that no one really likes you for who you are, that you'll never be able to meet the expectations of others... What does your body feel when shame speaks to you this way? What feelings can you surrender to the love of Jesus now?

Fours: As a Four, you likely feel the full intensity of shame (maybe even throughout your entire body) as it whispers to you that you'll never be understood and that no one can truly give you what you need/want. Can you present these difficult feelings to Jesus, as you acknowledge that he created you in all your uniqueness and that his love alone can make you feel truly understood?

Fives: As a Five, your primary way of feeling shame might be in your head. Perhaps its a buzzing sound that overwhelms and convinces you that you'll never have enough, you'll never know enough. Jesus' love can quiet this for you and replace those messages with the knowledge that you have all you need in Him. Invite this truth into your mind and body now.

Sixes: As a Six, shame and fear work together against you and against the calming reality of Jesus' love for you. You may feel your heart pounding in your chest, or maybe its the heat flush when shame tells you you're not safe and can't be certain of anything. The love Jesus has for you can remove your fears and give you comfort instead. Allow him to show you this today.

Sevens: As a Seven, it might be difficult to acknowledge where shame takes up residence within you. Perhaps it is felt in your belly as you try to consume experiences and excitement as a way to avoid pain. Often God uses our pain to teach about his immense love for us. Maybe that is one thing he wants to teach you or remind you of this advent season. How can you open yourself to this possibility?

Eights: As an Eight, shame might feel like an internal churning of helplessness and fear in your gut that you quickly want to mask over with anger and readiness to fight. As you learn to offer yourself to God this Advent season, will you allow God to help you see past this shame in order to let God to be your protector, shield, and Father who loves you?

Nines: As a Nine, love is the very thing for which you long. Shame for you may feel like an inability to move, a lack of motivation. Physically speaking, maybe it is a weight that presses down on you and tells you that you can't take up space or "impose" on others. Jesus' love draws you into action this advent. What does it feel like to imagine that weight being removed from your body and the love of God being poured over you?

Journaling Space

December 11

Luke 2:8-20

And in the same region there were shepherds out in the field, keeping watch over their flock by night. And an angel of the Lord appeared to them, and the glory of the Lord shone around them, and they were filled with great fear. And the angel said to them, "Fear not, for behold, I bring you good news of great joy that will be for all the people. For unto you is born this day in the city of David a Savior, who is Christ the Lord. And this will be a sign for you: you will find a baby wrapped in swaddling cloths and lying in a manger." And suddenly there was with the angel a multitude of the heavenly host praising God and saying,

"Glory to God in the highest,

and on earth peace among those with whom he is pleased!"

When the angels went away from them into heaven, the shepherds said to one another, "Let us go over to Bethlehem and see this thing that has happened, which the Lord has made known to us." And they went with haste and found Mary and Joseph, and the baby lying in a manger. And when they saw it, they made known the saying that had been told them concerning this child. And all who heard it wondered at what the shepherds told them. But Mary treasured up all these things, pondering them in her heart. And the shepherds returned, glorifying and praising God for all they had heard and seen, as it had been told them.

Reflection

During this time in history, shepherds were not exactly part of the top tier of society. They spent most of their time away from other people and with animals. They probably didn't really feel like part of the community in the same way many others did. Yet, in an act of love and grace God chose them to be the first ones to know the most wonderful news that had ever been proclaimed. Jesus was finally here! He could have just sent one angel to tell them, but because this was such a big deal and because he loved even the lowly shepherds, he gave them the full show! Not only that, he allowed them to experience community in a new way. These shepherds were undoubtedly bonded to each other through this. But they also had the privilege of telling others this exciting news and becoming a central part of the community in a unique way. Because God created us out of his love and to be in loving relationship with him and with others, love and community go hand in hand. When we experience God's love for us, it has the natural effect of driving us toward community because we want to share in this love with others. How are you experiencing God's love in your life currently and in what ways is God leading you to share it with your community?

Moving to Action

Ones: When you truly believe and feel God's love for you, you are free to accept your own imperfections as well as the imperfection of the people and world around you. As you experience this Christmas season with your community, how might God's love extend through you to others in acceptance and grace?

Twos: When you truly believe and feel God's love for you, you are free to acknowledge and ask for what you need. As you experience this Christmas season with your community, how might God change the way you interact with yourself and those around you in regard to needs?

Threes: When you truly believe and feel God's love for you, you are free to take off any masks and be your true self. As you experience this Christmas season with your community, how will laying down your facades and need for success enable you to better love others?

Fours: When you truly believe and feel God's love for you, you are free to find contentment in who God made you to be. As you experience this Christmas season with your community, how might this contentment shape the way you engage with others?

Fives: When you truly believe and feel God's love for you, you are free to deeply connect with others. As you experience this Christmas season with your community, how might God's love propel you into deep relationship and enable you to offer yourself to others?

Sixes: When you truly believe and feel God's love for you, you are free to trust yourself and others. As you experience this Christmas season with your community, how might this trust help you enjoy the present moment and be a pillar of strength for others?

Sevens: When you truly believe and feel God's love for you, you are free to engage pain and discomfort. As you experience this Christmas season with your community, how might God's love enable you to offer others a safe place to walk through grief, sorrow, and heartache?

Eights: When you truly believe and feel God's love for you, you are free to be vulnerable and childlike. As you experience this Christmas season with your community, how might God's love flow out into a joyful celebration that invites others in?

Nines: When you truly believe and feel God's love for you, you are free to be seen and valued. As you experience this Christmas season with your community, how might God's love motivate you to be an active part of the lives of others?

Journaling Space

December 12

Psalm 46:10

"Be still and know that I am God. I will be exalted among the nations, I will be exalted in the earth!"

Today is a day for resting in the knowledge of God and reflecting on his love. Take a few minutes to quiet your mind, your heart, and your body. Imagine holding yourself up to the warmth of the light of God in order to fully experience God's love. Spend a few moments there, taking in all that God has to offer you today.

Joy

This week, we'll focus our attention on the theme of Joy. As we explore our beliefs, feelings, and actions together, allow yourself to stay centered on the idea of joy and in what ways you need to experience Christ's joy this Christmas.

December 13

Micah 5:2
But you, O Bethlehem Ephrathah,
Who are too little to be among the clans of Judah, From you shall come forth for me
One who is to be ruler in Israel, Whose coming is from old,
From ancient of days.

Reflection
Have you ever felt like you somehow just don't fit? Maybe you're too young, maybe you're too old, maybe you're of a minority group, maybe you're of a different socioeconomic status, maybe you have different interests or talents than others near you. We could think of a thousand things that make us feel like we don't fit or belong. The one thing we have in common though is that every single one of us doubts (or has doubted) our belonging in some way, shape, or form. As the prophet Micah spoke on behalf of God about Bethlehem, he offered the promise of belonging and of purpose. Though a tiny little "nothing" town, it was promised that the greatest ruler ever, the one who had been spoken of and promised to God's people for ages would come from this place. A promise that God would not allow Bethlehem to continue in its "unbelonging" but rather would give it meaning and purpose. God has the same promise for each of us- He will give us belonging and purpose. Advent is a unique time to reflect on our sense of belonging and purpose. What do these reflections stir in you? Does thinking about belonging and purpose bring you heartache or joy?

Exploring Belief

Ones: Perhaps you hold the belief that your belonging and purpose come from being perfect or having the ability to fix the problems around you. If this is true for you, Jesus offers a different kind of purpose, one defined by his unmerited favor for you. Belonging to him brings joy rather than obligation. What would it require of you to submit to this kind of belonging and purpose?

Twos: Purpose for you may feel rooted in what you have to give to others so that they need you and love you. Jesus has a very different message for you. He does not need you, but rather chooses you, wants you and delights in you because you are his. You belong to him. How does this truth strike you today?

Threes: Your sense of belonging or purpose is most likely contingent on what others think of you and how successful you are perceived to be. If you can do enough dances, wear enough hats, climb enough rungs on the ladder, you're set! Perhaps today Jesus is asking you to trade in your striving and hiding for the joy that comes from being accepted for who you are, rather than what you can do.

Fours: As a Four, you may feel the least sense of belonging. It can feel hard to "fit" when you feel so misunderstood. The beautiful thing is that because God made you, he never misunderstands you. He knows you intimately and sees such beauty in you. Ask yourself if there is anything keeping you from accepting this as truth and embracing Christ's joy today.

Fives: At first glance, the idea of belonging may not feel all that important to you as you are comfortable and content with your internal world. Yet we know that you too were made for community and to belong to Christ and his body. What do you believe about your purpose within community? Can you find joy in sharing in the knowledge of Christ and trusting his omniscience over his purpose for you?

Sixes: Belonging may feel both very important and very scary for you. You desperately want to be able to trust and yet you also constantly find yourself anticipating the worst. This push-pull in your heart and mind is exhausting. What would it be like to rest in the belonging and purpose God gives you as his child? How might that free you to experience joy in your life?

Sevens: Belonging might not seem that difficult for you on the surface. You're the life of the party, always up for an adventure, and able to keep people entertained. If you stop and think about it, do you ever feel lonely or disconnected because of this drive to keep moving? Does that impact your sense of belonging or purpose? Jesus came so that you might find your place in him and if you allow yourself to belong to him, he promises to give you everything you need. What is in the way of you consenting to this during this season?

Eights: It is next to impossible to experience joy and belonging when you are constantly trying to protect yourself from others and maintain self-sufficiency. And yet the childlike part of you desperately wants to feel the joy that comes from freely engaging with others and the world around you. What would it require of you to let yourself truly belong to another? What tries to prevent you from trusting God with your belonging and your purpose?

Nines: In a way, you may feel like you belong to everybody and nobody at the same time. You're able to interact with all different kinds of people and understand all different sorts of perspectives. Yet, the one place you might not feel like you belong is within yourself. What would you need to hear from Jesus today to remind you that he gives you belonging and purpose because he delights in who you are?

Journaling Space

December 14

Luke 2:1-6
In those days a decree went out from Caesar Augustus that all the world should be registered. This was the first registration when Quirinius was governor of Syria. And all went to be registered, each to his own town. And Joseph also went up from Galilee, from the town of Nazareth, to Judea, to the city of David, which is called Bethlehem, because he was of the house and lineage of David, to be registered with Mary, his betrothed, who was with child. And while they were there, the time came for her to give birth.

Reflection
Imagine this progression of events and, if you can, place yourself in the story as an on-looker, or even as one of the main characters. Everyone is required to participate in a census so that the government can keep track of its people. This means Joseph has to travel back to his hometown, but by this point Mary is very far along in her pregnancy. Together, they have to travel extremely far, while Mary is extremely pregnant, and then while away from the comfort of home (and in a barn no less!), Mary goes into labor and gives birth to Jesus. What a challenging and stressful experience this must have been for them. Yet somehow God always seems to come through in these kinds of situations. He takes life experiences that are difficult and stressful, and somehow brings about joy. In the midst of all the crazy- the travel, the sleeping with animals, the labor- he brings Jesus into the world and gives Mary, Joseph, and everyone else the greatest gift ever! What difficulties are you facing this Advent season? Is it possible God will bring about joy for you in the midst of your own struggles?

Exploring Belief

Ones: It is clear that there was nothing Joseph and Mary could have done to "fix" their situation or make it seem more in line with what is considered "right" by most. For Ones, joy can seem hard to come by in such challenging situations. Your drive to fix and make things right likely takes over and prevents you from seeing the joy that may be brought about by the act of surrendering to God's plan. What challenging situations are you facing in your life? Can you practice surrendering to God's perfection and his joy in the midst of chaos?

Twos: The omnipotent God takes on a vulnerable role as he enters into the world. He comes as an innocent, defenseless baby who is utterly dependent on Mary and Joseph to provide all his needs. And even now, he continues to invite humanity to play an essential role in bringing him afresh to this world. God trusted Mary and Joseph to care for His own beloved Son. And today, God chooses you to bring his power, presence and love into this world. Put into words a prayer of gratitude toward the God who loves you and chooses you today.

Threes: To all outside perspectives, the birth of Jesus Christ was a disaster: born out of wedlock, rejected at the inn, and birthed into a feeding trough surrounded by farm animals. The God of all creation entered the world in total humility. Jesus was free to choose this path because his identity is firmly rooted in his relationship with God the Father. How is God inviting you to find joy in your relationship with him this season? Ask God, "who do you say I am today?"

Fours: When Jesus was born, the entire sum of God's beauty, power, brilliance, and holiness found its home in human flesh. This mystery is beyond human comprehension and reaches to the depth of our very being. In the Incarnation, God elevated the status of human flesh, choosing to dwell among us. And he still dwells with us to this day. Can you find the joy of participating in God's mysterious and beautiful fellowship with you this Advent season? Can you take a few minutes today to simply be with him and know his great desire for you?

Fives: By entering into humanity's time and space, God reached past the barriers of mystery and glory to make himself known, revealing to us true knowledge and fellowship. Jesus made the invisible God tangible, real and knowable. As you reflect on the image of Jesus entering into our world, how does that fill you with joy? Can you draw near to the newborn Savior and soak in the joy of seeing his face?

Sixes: In a world that stirs up constant anxiety and fear, Jesus came to bring eternal, lasting, tangible peace. Through the series of wild events that led to his birth, we learn that even in the most chaotic times, God will weave together ultimate good for those who love him. As you meditate on Jesus' presence among us, how is God inviting you toward joy and away from fear? Can you surrender knowing that your Savior is with you here and now?

Sevens: By conventional human standards, Jesus' entry into the world was far from perfect. Yet in God's perfect wisdom, this was the path that he saw as perfectly fitting. And given all the power in the universe, God chose this humble path to introduce the world to the exalted Son. As you look around your world, can you find joy knowing that God has chosen this life for you? Can you find less importance on temporary circumstances, and instead find ultimate joy in the God who deeply desires to be with you today?

Eights: Eights fight to control the world around them. Imagine how many times Joseph and Mary felt like they were not in control. They could not control the census, the accommodations, or even their birth experience. Yet, as the sounds of baby Jesus' cries echoed through the darkness of Bethlehem that night, all their frustrations and fears dimmed in the joy of their son. How can the voice of the Savior refocus your attention toward joy rather than fear this season? What is the Savior saying to you today?

Nines: Each baby that enters into the world is utterly unique to their parents. The subtle details of their face, voice, and personality are treasured by mother and fathers who spend countless hours soaking in every unique detail. As a Nines, can you embrace the truth that God loves you as much as he loved his Son, Jesus? Can you find joy that God sees your face, knows your desires and your heart, and is greatly pleased with you? Contemplation has been described as looking back into God's gaze, and seeing his delight in you. Will you take time to enjoy the God who always holds you as the apple of His eye?

Journaling Space

December 15

Zephaniah 3:14-17
Sing aloud, O daughter of Zion; shout, O Israel! Rejoice and exult with all your heart, O daughter of Jerusalem! The Lord has taken away the judgments against you; he has cleared away your enemies. The King of Israel, the Lord, is in your midst; you shall never again fear evil. On that day it shall be said to Jerusalem: "Fear not, O Zion; let not your hands grow weak. The Lord your God is in your midst, a mighty one who will save; he will rejoice over you with gladness; he will quiet you by his love; he will exult over you with loud singing.

Reflection
As Christians, we often think about our own personal experience of joy. But how often have you considered God's joy? Since we are image-bearers of him, our qualities mirror his, no matter how dimly or poorly. While happiness is a temporary emotion, joy is an internal characteristic, or state of being, that finds its source in God. It is not something we can muster on our own or rely on circumstances to provide for us. Instead it comes from God to and through us. And even more than that, God finds joy in us! He rejoices over us because we are His! He has given us his characteristics and has demonstrated to us how to enact those characteristics. Imagine what it looks like when God rejoices over you. What images come to mind and how do those images impact you?

Engaging Feeling

Eights, Nines, & Ones: Take a few minutes to remember times that you have felt joyful. As best as you can, connect with these memories in a tangible way. What does joy feel like in your body? Where does it take its residence? Is there anything that wants to stop you from experiencing joy today? Acknowledge all these things before God today, asking that His joy would be what fills you now.

Twos, Threes, and Fours: There are many heart-centered words in today's Scripture: "Rejoice and exult with all your heart," "you shall never again fear," "rejoice...with gladness...". The feelings associated with joy are powerful and meaningful and God not only feels them, he feels them for you! Allow that truth to take root in your heart in a new way today. God rejoices over you and imparts to you the same joy he has. What do you want to say to him in response?

Fives, Sixes, & Sevens: Joy. What comes into your mind when you read that word or say it aloud to yourself? Are your thoughts filled with memories, or perhaps with a sense of longing? Whatever it is, spend some time writing down these associations your brain makes. When you are finished, ask God to give you his joy to fill your thoughts.

December 16

Luke 1:46-55
And Mary said, "My soul magnifies the Lord,
and my spirit rejoices in God my Savior, for he has looked on the humble estate of his servant.
For behold, from now on all generations will call me blessed; for he who is mighty has done great things for me,
and holy is his name.
And his mercy is for those who fear him
from generation to generation.
He has shown strength with his arm;
he has scattered the proud in the thoughts of their hearts; he has brought down the mighty from their thrones
and exalted those of humble estate; he has filled the hungry with good things,
and the rich he has sent away empty. He has helped his servant Israel,
in remembrance of his mercy, as he spoke to our fathers,
to Abraham and to his offspring forever."

Reflection
This was Mary's song of adoration and celebration about the amazing things she was seeing and experiencing as God fulfilled thousands of years of promises right in front of her eyes and within her womb. When Mary saw in a new way who God is, how he had chosen her and that she could rest in the work He was doing, there was nothing left to do but celebrate! When was the last time you allowed yourself to celebrate in this way? What would it feel like to know this kind of joy this Advent season?

Engaging Feeling

How can you intentionally engage in joyful celebration like Mary did?

Ones: Find three things today that exist in the world that bring you joy, just as they are without needing alteration or upgrading. Offer thanks to God for the gift of his goodness in the world.

Twos: Give a small gift or another expression of love to yourself without condition or guilt, as though it is from God. Allow yourself to feel joyful about receiving such a gift. Offer thanks to God for the gift of his love in the world.

Threes: Take time to seek out something that proves to you that God is enduring and holds all things together so you don't have to. Allow yourself to feel the joy that comes from not needing to be the one to accomplish it all and thank God for this gift.

Fours: Find and acknowledge three things that are mysteriously beautiful about yourself or the world around you and allow yourself to delight in them. Offer thanks to God for the gift of his beauty in the world.

Fives: Find something that feels delightfully incomprehensible to you- music, space, human complexity- and revel in not needing to have all the answers to enjoy it. Offer thanks to God for the gift of his knowledge in the world.

Sixes: Go to a place where you have experienced the fullness of God's presence (in nature, by a fire, in a church…) and bask in the joy and security his presence gives you. Offer thanks to God for the gift of his presence in the world.

Sevens: Remind yourself of several ways over the past year that God has satisfied your needs and even your desires. Allow the joy that comes with God's good gifts to ground you in the present moment so you can fully experience what he has done. Offer thanks to God for the gift of his provision in the world.

Eights: Think of a time when you felt safe and free to feel. Engage the childlike part of yourself and dance or play or skip with joy. Offer thanks to God for the gift of his protection in the world.

Nines: Acknowledge at least three things that are unique and valuable about yourself. Celebrate these things by sharing them with a safe person in your life. Offer thanks to God for the gift of his image in the world.

Journaling Space

December 17

Matthew 2:9-11
After listening to the king, they went on their way. And behold, the star that they had seen when it rose went before them until it came to rest over the place where the child was. When they saw the star, they rejoiced exceedingly with great joy. And going into the house, they saw the child with Mary his mother, and they fell down and worshiped him. Then, opening their treasures, they offered him gifts, gold, frankincense, and myrrh.

Reflection
Have you ever pursued something for an extended period of time? Weeks, months, years even? When you finally reached it, what did you do? Most people celebrate in some way to mark their accomplishment, hard work, and commitment that has finally paid off. And some celebrate as a sign of relief that they have finished. Perhaps this is somewhat similar to what the wise men experienced. After researching, charting, and watching the sky, they finally find the star for which they have been looking. Then, after traveling hundreds of miles over the course of what was probably weeks following this star, they finally see its stopping point. What joy (and maybe some relief) must have filled their hearts in that moment! The thing they had been pursuing for so long was just on the other side of the door to the house! They had found the long-promised kings of the Jews! It's possible their rejoicing was for their accomplishment, or out of relief that their journey was coming to an end. But more than likely the joy they felt was, at its core, the deep satisfaction of seeing God fulfill his promises. What promises has God fulfilled in your life and what are you still hoping for from him?

Moving to Action

Yesterday we practiced feeling joy for ourselves. Today let's look at how we can share that joy with others.

Threes, Sevens, & Eights: As active energy types[1], expressing joy (when you have it) might feel relatively natural to you. It's been said that joy is contagious. What are some ways that you can share your joyful active energy with others? How can you display your joy in a way that Invites others to join you in your celebration of our Savior?

Fours, Fives, & Nines: As receptive types, the joy you display might look a little quieter or even sit deeper than those with active energy. However, it is no less effective and no less important. In what ways can your unique expression of joy be used to help others find joy? Can you use this deep and quiet joy to bring others who might be struggling into the joy of Christmas?

Ones, Twos, & SIxes: As balancing energy types, you have the ability to know what is needed and move toward that need. As you interact with others today, pay attention to what kind of joy they might need. Perhaps one person needs the freedom to burst into joyful laughter. Perhaps another needs a quiet appreciation for kindness shown in their life. Wherever you go, and whomever you meet, trust yourself to interject the kind of joy that others might need today.

December 18

Psalm 46:10
"Be still and know that I am God. I will be exalted among the nations, I will be exalted in the earth!"

Today is a day for resting in the knowledge of God and reflecting on his joy. Take a few minutes to quiet your mind, your heart, and your body. Imagine holding yourself up to the warmth of the light of God in order to fully experience God's joy. Spend a few moments there, taking in all that God has to offer you today.

Hope

This week, we'll focus our attention on the theme of Hope. As we explore our beliefs, feelings, and actions together, allow yourself to stay centered on the idea of hope and in what ways you need to experience Christ's hope this Christmas.

December 19

Isaiah 61:1-3
The Spirit of the Lord God is upon me, because the Lord has anointed me to bring good news to the poor; he has sent me to bind up the brokenhearted, to proclaim liberty to the captives, and the opening of the prison to those who are bound; to proclaim the year of the Lord's favor, and the day of vengeance of our God; to comfort all who mourn; to grant to those who mourn in Zion— to give them a beautiful headdress instead of ashes, the oil of gladness instead of mourning, the garment of praise instead of a faint spirit; that they may be called oaks of righteousness, the planting of the Lord, that he may be glorified

Reflection
This Old Testament prophecy sums up all of what Jesus came to do. When he was born as a baby into this world, his purpose was to fulfill this prophecy and in doing so, offer the hope of eternal life to all those who should choose to follow him. And even more than that, those of us who believe and follow him have the opportunity to live out his mission and bring about God's kingdom by doing the very things Jesus did. As ambassadors of Christ, we too can bring good news to the poor, bind up the brokenhearted, proclaim liberty to the captives, proclaim the year of the Lord's favor and of his perfect vengeance, and comfort those who mourn. It's difficult to find something that offers this much hope for us all, and yet here it is. It was wrapped up in a tiny baby who changed the world forever by giving himself to it and for it. In what areas of your life are you needing to experience or express hope?

Exploring Belief

Where do you find hope?

Ones: You may find hope in seeing everything made "right." This advent, can you find hope in the reality that you do not have to accomplish this and that God will (even if his ways do not make complete sense to you)?

Twos: Hope for you might come in the form of feeling loved and wanted by people in your life to whom you have shown great love. This Advent, can you find hope in the reality that Jesus loves you without reservation or condition? He sees your broken heart and has come to bind it up.

Threes: Is hope found in accomplishments and proving that you are worthwhile? This Advent, Jesus wants to offer you the freedom that comes from finding hope in him and his immovability.

Fours: Perhaps hope for you is found in your ability to feel deeply or intensely. Yet this also means that you are prone to despair, feeling as though no one could truly grasp your experience of life. What would mean for you to set aside this melancholy outlook and find lightness in the hope that Jesus knows your innermost thoughts and feelings?

Fives: You likely are prone to find hope in your unending search for knowledge, always feeling like you need more information to be sure. Jesus' challenge for you this advent is to remember that his incarnation brings the full integration of intellect, emotion, and environment, so that you can rest in the mystery of God. What beliefs do you hold that prevent you from surrendering yourself to this mystery?

Sixes: Does hope for you result from having a contingency plan and therefore the ability to keep yourself safe? Consider that Jesus did not prioritize his own safety when he became flesh, but rather loved you so much that he disregarded his own security to save you. How can you embrace his willingness to risk everything for you as the thing that gives you hope?

Sevens: You may find hope in looking ahead to the next thing on your calendar, the next mountain to climb, the next party to attend, the next project to start. This Advent, can you accept the realized hope of Jesus incarnate as the ultimate fulfillment of everything you could ever need?

Eights: Hope for you might come from your sense of vengeance, your ability to exact retribution for yourself or for others who appear to be weak and vulnerable. Interact with the idea that God chose to save the world through innocence and gentleness- an infant- rather than war horses and soldiers. How can you find rest in the kind of hope Jesus offers you?

Nines: Perhaps for you the idea of hope feels evasive. If you're accustomed to flying under the radar, hope might not be something you've often thought about, or felt allowed to think about having for yourself. This Advent, Jesus offers you hope through the harmony he brings to the world. Can you embrace this truth as the thing that frees you to be present and active in your own life?

Journaling Space

December 20

Romans 5:1-5
Therefore, since we have been justified by faith, we have peace with God through our Lord Jesus Christ. Through him we have also obtained access by faith into this grace in which we stand, and we rejoice in hope of the glory of God. Not only that, but we rejoice in our sufferings, knowing that suffering produces endurance, and endurance produces character, and character produces hope, and hope does not put us to shame, because God's love has been poured into our hearts through the Holy Spirit who has been given to us.

Reflection
Many of us spend a good chunk of our time trying to avoid suffering altogether or, at the very least, quickly escape the suffering we inevitably experience. What would happen if our perspective on suffering shifted to fall in line with what we have just read? What if we truly believed that the suffering we experience was going to lead us to hope? And not a "wishful thinking" kind of hope, but a true understanding that God has us and will not allow our suffering to destroy us ("put us to shame"). This would not make our suffering any more pleasant or even easier to actually walk through. It would, however, change both our perceived ability to endure and the meaning we assign to our suffering. This is undeniably part of the Christian faith. It is promised that we will suffer (John 16:33, 2 Tim. 3:12) and it is promised that our suffering will be worthwhile (1 Peter 5:10, 2 Cor. 4:17, Rom. 8:18). If it weren't for this hope, we would crumble under the weight of tragedy, loss, disappointment, physical pain, betrayal… Many choose not to acknowledge or engage their suffering, especially at Christmastime. But since suffering leads to hope and Advent is about hope, this seems like a prime time to acknowledge our suffering and look toward the hope that only Jesus can bring about for us. Give yourself the space and time to do this now. What kind of suffering are your currently experiencing and what do you want to ask Jesus to do with this suffering?

Exploring Belief

Ones: How do you cope with suffering? Is it through anger and resentment? By trying to create order out of the pain and the chaos? Acknowledge and lay down these coping strategies today and embrace the hope only Jesus can bring about.

Twos: How do you cope with suffering? Is it through the pride and distraction that comes from taking care of others? Do you busy your mlnd and heart with the positive feelings associated with loving and meeting the needs of someone else? Acknowledge and lay down these coping strategies today and embrace the hope only Jesus can bring about.

Threes: How do you cope with suffering? Is it through deceiving yourself and others that everything is ok? By focusing on the appearance of things in order to keep moving forward? Acknowledge and lay down these coping strategies today and embrace the hope only Jesus can bring about.

Fours: How do you cope with suffering? Is it by relinquishing yourself to depressed feelings and wondering why the world is so unfair? By looking at others and wondering why you seem to suffer more than they do? Acknowledge and lay down these coping strategies today and embrace the hope only Jesus can bring about.

Fives: How do you cope with suffering? Is it by withdrawing into yourself so you can find the answer to your suffering on your own? By trying to drown out the noise and get through it alone? Acknowledge and lay down these coping strategies today and embrace the hope only Jesus can bring about.

Sixes: How do you cope with suffering? Is it through fear and anxiety? Do you try to hide from the suffering or even push against it as a way to get it over with more quickly? Acknowledge and lay down these coping strategies today and embrace the hope only Jesus can bring about.

Sevens: How do you cope with suffering? Is it by looking to the future, the next high or pleasure you might experience? Do you look away from suffering hoping you can move on from it if you don't pay it too much attention? Acknowledge and lay down these coping strategies today and embrace the hope only Jesus can bring about.

Eights: How do you cope with suffering? Is it through lust and vengeance? Do you seek payback and someone to blame for what is occurring? Acknowledge and lay down these coping strategies today and embrace the hope only Jesus can bring about.

Nines: How do you cope with suffering? Is it by giving up and checking out? Do you become unmotivated, lazy even as you allow the hardship to cripple you? Acknowledge and lay down these coping strategies today and embrace the hope only Jesus can bring about.

Journaling Space

December 21

Psalm 130:5-8
I wait for the Lord, my soul waits,
and in his word I hope; my soul waits for the Lord
more than watchmen for the morning,
more than watchmen for the morning. O Israel, hope in the Lord!
For with the Lord there is steadfast love,
and with him is plentiful redemption. And he will redeem Israel
from all his iniquities.

Reflection
Waiting... Advent is all about waiting for the arrival of Jesus. Waiting can often feel like inaction, sitting around doing nothing, biding time until something happens. This passage, though, likens waiting for the Lord to watchmen waiting for the morning. Watchmen were responsible for keeping lookout throughout the night in order to protect the town and sound the alarm in the event of an attack from an enemy. This was not a "doing" sort of job as much as it was a "being" sort of job. It's not hard to imagine that after a full night of vigilance, with the safety of the city in your hands, that waiting for the sun to rise would be a very active sort of waiting. It's also not hard to imagine a sort of relief coming over the watchmen once the sun did rise. This Advent what would it be like to consistently wait on the Lord in this way, as though your very life depends on him? This is not a passive waiting, but an active and engaged sort of waiting. Will you allow yourself to experience this "being" kind of waiting?

Engaging Feeling

Ones: What are you waiting for from Jesus this Advent season? Do you notice your tendency to want to take matters into your own hands? Today, take a minute to kneel as a sign of dependence and set your heart on waiting on God. Surrender to being, rather than doing and wait for the Lord to shine on you, giving you his hope for your future.

Twos: As you think about times where you have waited on the Lord, do you notice yourself feeling the need to give something in order to get what you wanted/needed from him? Can you allow Jesus's hope to fill your heart this Advent, knowing that you do not have to create an equal exchange scenario in order to be loved and cherished?

Threes: What does it feel like for you to be still and wait? Because of your achiever nature, waiting may feel somewhat like torture as you are driven to prove yourself in order to advance. This Advent, can you invite the hope Jesus offers you to cover over your feelings of inadequacy and worthlessness? As you pray, allow yourself to feel the hope of Jesus fill your soul.

Fours: Its likely a common experience for you to quickly move from one emotion to the next, and to feel each emotion deeply. This Advent season, Jesus wants to offer you something new to be the undercurrent of all the emotion you feel: hope. Hope that your feelings are valid and purposeful, hope that you are uniquely valued by God, and hope that he came to this earth for you. What is it like to sink into this kind of hope?

Fives: When was the last time you waited expectantly for something and what did this feel like? Perhaps waiting is tied to feelings of emptiness or ambiguity for you. What would it be like to know and trust that Jesus always delivers on his promises and will never leave you helpless and wandering without hope?

Sixes: Waiting may feel directly linked to uncertainty and is likely tinged with fear for you. What are you waiting on right now and how is your anxiety coloring that waiting? Can you share your feelings of fear or anxiety with Jesus and allow him to replace those feelings with his expectant hope?

Sevens: The feeling of waiting likely sometimes feels unbearable for you. Rather than waiting expectantly, you would prefer to distract yourself with something else- your own form of passive waiting. What would happen if you allowed yourself to sit in stillness expectantly waiting for God to provide whatever it is you're needing from him this advent season? Challenge yourself to try this.

Eights: How do you feel about waiting? Perhaps impatient? Perhaps irritated? For you, a major component of waiting on God includes trusting his control and his timing for things, even when it is not the way you would do things. If you can do this, you can find hope in him rather than in your drive to exact justice for yourself and others. What would this kind of waiting feel like for you?

Nines: In truth, waiting might not feel that difficult for you. You're pretty well acquainted with going with the flow and seeing what happens. This advent, Jesus's challenge for you is to become more active in your waiting. What would it feel like to eagerly look for what Jesus has for you and who he is calling you to be rather than allowing facets of your life to just happen?

Journaling Space

December 22

John 1:14
And the Word became flesh and dwelt among us, and we have seen his glory, glory as of the only Son from the Father, full of grace and truth.

Reflection
As we near the end of this Advent season let us again be reminded of the hope we have in Jesus. When he put on human flesh and walked this earth, he gave us an incredible gift. He showed us his glory- who he truly is. And perhaps included in this was an invitation for us to show him (and ourselves) who we are so that we might be in true, intimate, fully-known relationship with him. This is why Jesus came. We were separated from God because of sin and shame, unable to make our own way back to him. It was necessary for him to become like us to show us the way. Part of that way back involves us becoming vulnerable, unveiling our true selves to him, so that we can fully embrace him and be fully embraced by him. We must stop hiding from God, as we started doing so long ago in the Garden, so that he can give us the life he intended for us. There is no greater hope than this.

Engaging Feeling

Threes, Sevens, & Eights: The Future-Focused Types[2]: By focusing on the future, you are able to keep yourself from being vulnerable in the present and liable for your past. You avoid the present discomfort that comes from recalling past mistakes or painful experiences. Today, allow yourself to remain in the present moment. Center yourself where you are by taking several deep breaths and allow yourself to connect with what is happening internally for you right now. Talk to God about these things.

Ones, Twos, & Sixes: The Present-Focused Types: By focusing on the present, you convince yourself of your ability to mitigate any potential harm due to vulnerability in the future. Staying focused on the task at hand feels as though it protects you from ever repeating past mistakes or feeling disappointed when the future does not turn out as you had hoped. Allow yourself to imagine a bright future for yourself. Engage this kind of vulnerability as you dream and hope. Share these hopes and dreams with Jesus now.

Fours, Fives, & Nines: The Past-Focused Types: By focusing on the past, you retreat into yourself and avoid interacting with the present moment, which requires vulnerability. Rather than longing for or fixating on what was or what could have been, can you choose in this moment to feel the reality of now? Can you present yourself to God as you are now and embrace his current reality for you?

December 23

Luke 1:67-79
And his father Zechariah was filled with the Holy Spirit and prophesied, saying, "Blessed be the Lord God of Israel, for he has visited and redeemed his people and has raised up a horn of salvation for us in the house of his servant David, as he spoke by the mouth of his holy prophets from of old, that we should be saved from our enemies and from the hand of all who hate us; to show the mercy promised to our fathers and to remember his holy covenant, the oath that he swore to our father Abraham, to grant us that we, being delivered from the hand of our enemies, might serve him without fear, in holiness and righteousness before him all our days. And you, child, will be called the prophet of the Most High; for you will go before the Lord to prepare his ways, to give knowledge of salvation to his people in the forgiveness of their sins, because of the tender mercy of our God, whereby the sunrise shall visit us from on high to give light to those who sit in darkness and in the shadow of death, to guide our feet into the way of peace."

Reflection
John the Baptist was a harbinger of hope. He, according to Jesus, was the greatest Old Testament prophet who ever lived. In the Gospels, there are no recorded miracles performed by John. His exalted status as prophet has less to do with flashy miracles and more to do with his proximity to Jesus. This Advent season, we are invited to turn away from our accomplishments and worldly importance and instead bask in the glory of our proximity to Jesus. The Incarnation did not end when Jesus took on flesh, but it continues in you today- in your heart, in your soul, in your mind. It is Christ in you, the hope of glory. How can you bring this into the world today?

Moving to Action

Each type has within themselves a holy virtue[3], which represents the best parts of ourselves as God created us to be. This is a unique way we bring hope into this world. Reflect on your type-specific holy virtue as you prepare to celebrate the birth of Jesus and continue his mission in the world.

Ones: The holy virtue of the One is Serenity. Jesus embodied and offered to others shalom- perfectly satisfied soul-level peace. How can you represent the serenity of Jesus to those around you in order to facilitate peace in a very chaotic world?

Twos: The holy virtue of the Two is Humility. Jesus was the most humble of all servants. How can you display the same humility Jesus did to those around you? And how might your humility prompt others to respond with curiosity toward who Jesus really is?

Threes: The holy virtue for the Three is Truthfulness. Jesus was (of course) truthful, even when it was unpopular to be so. In what ways can you embody truthfulness to those around you as a way to invite them into truthful relationship with God and others?

Fours: The holy virtue for the Four is Equanimity- the ability to hold all emotions in balance. Jesus, as the origination point of all emotion, knows the depths and experience of emotion wholly. How can you use your ability to feel and understand emotions deeply as a way to reflect Jesus's heart for people?

Fives: The holy virtue for the Five is Detachment, not needing to hold on to the things of this world and the answers that lie within it. Jesus embodied detachment each time he prayed "Not my will but yours be done." In what ways can you embrace this detachment in order to point others to the mystery of salvation offered through Jesus?

Sixes: The holy virtue for the Six is Courage. Jesus's courage enabled him to eat with tax collectors, prostitutes, and other "sinners." How can this same courage calm your inner anxiety and move you into relationships with others that point to Jesus?

Sevens: The holy virtue for the Seven is Sobriety (or sober-mindedness). Jesus gave us a perfect example of a sober-minded life in which he was constantly looking to fulfill his Father's will. How might your sober-minded living impact those around you and direct them toward who God is or desires to be in their lives?

 Eights: The holy virtue for the Eight is Innocence. Jesus, being born as a helpless baby and then living life completely without sin is the perfect picture of innocence. How might you embrace this innocence and invite others into a holy life with God?

Nines: The holy virtue for the Nine is Action. The life of Jesus is full of action- healing the sick, casting out demons, going toe-to-toe with the religious leaders of his time- and all because of his love for his people. How might you exemplify this love in action as you seek to represent Jesus to those around you?

Journaling Space

December 24

Psalm 46:10 "Be still and know that I am God. I will be exalted among the nations, I will be exalted in the earth!"

Merry Christmas Eve! Today is a day for resting in the knowledge of God and reflecting on all the themes we have explored this Advent season- peace, love, joy and hope. Take a few minutes to quiet your mind, your heart, and your body. Imagine holding yourself up to the warmth of the light of God in order to fully experience God, as he is. Spend a few moments there, taking in all that God has to offer you today and prepare your heart for Christmas day when you remember and welcome Jesus into your world.

[1] The Enneagram has been studied and grouped according to triads based on commonalities regarding emotion centers, orientation to time, energy expression, etc. This week's grouping and terminology is adopted from http://drdaviddaniels.com/articles/triads/

[2] This week's triad grouping and terminology is adopted from https://ieaninepoints.com/2019/02/01/the-enneagram-and-the-fullness-of-time/#!biz/id/5b58cfd8f033bfaf49d554d6

[3] This way of describing holy virtues is adopted from The Sacred Enneagram by Chris Heuertz

Made in the USA
San Bernardino, CA
25 November 2019